I0166095

P. P. Henson

The armenian amphitheater and its bloody arena

P. P. Henson

The armenian amphitheater and its bloody arena

ISBN/EAN: 9783743377097

Manufactured in Europe, USA, Canada, Australia, Japa

Cover: Foto ©ninafisch / pixelio.de

Manufactured and distributed by brebook publishing software
(www.brebook.com)

P. P. Henson

The armenian amphitheater and its bloody arena

The Armenian Amphitheater

And its Bloody Arena.

A ZEIBECK.

THE STORY
IN A NUTSHELL

BY A

TWENTY YEARS' RESIDENT
OF TURKEY.

INTRODUCTION BY

REV. P. S. HENSON, D. D.

CHICAGO, NEW YORK, TORONTO :
FLEMING H. REVELL CO.

400,000 People Are Starving.

If you wish to help these people send contributions to the **Armenian Relief Committee,** E. G. Keith, Treasurer, Metropolitan National Bank, Chicago.

One dollar will feed one person three months.

THE

Armenian Amphitheater

AND ITS BLOODY ARENA.

BY A
TWENTY YEARS' RESIDENT OF TURKEY.

INTRODUCTION BY
REV. P. S. HENSON, D. D.

———— ————

FLEMING H. REVELL COMPANY,
CHICAGO.   NEW YORK.   TORONTO.
Publishers of Evangelical Literature.

ARMENIAN VICTIMS OF THE MASSACRES.

Copyright, 1896,
By Fleming H. Revell Co.

INTRODUCTION.

NEVER since the time when Christians were fed to the lions in Roman arenas, and in their shirts of tar burned like candles in Nero's Gardens, have such diabolical persecutions been witnessed as are now being enacted by fanatical Moslems within the bounds of the Ottoman Empire, and within sight, and also within easy reach, of all the great powers of Europe, that call themselves Christian. Yet, to their eternal shame, these content themselves with uttering mild-mannered diplomatic protests, instead of laying an iron hand upon the perpetrators of these infamies and saying in thunder tones: "These butcheries must be stopped, or, as there is a God in heaven and any justice left on earth, your blood shall atone for every drop of blood that you shed." The European powers are under special obligations to take this stand for God and for humanity, because, by reason of their proximity, they can strike effectively as well as speak authoritatively. And they are not only under special obligations, but they have an especial right, in view of the fact that the Sultan, by whose connivance or command these atrocities are perpetrated, is thereby trampling upon sacred treaties made with these same European powers, and, there-fore, every consideration of justice and humanity alike demands that an end be put to a condition of things that has come to be intolerable. And yet, the fact

3

is only too palpably and painfully apparent that the rulers of Europe are more concerned about the partitioning of Turkey than about the persecution of Christians; that they have a deeper interest in Turkish bonds, in which they have millions invested, than in Armenian blood, with which Turkish scimiters are daily dripping. Just what may be the duty of America in this solemn exigency is a question that is painfully exercising many thoughtful minds and troubling many sensitive consciences.

Whatever may be thought of the Monroe doctrine, we can not in isolated selfishness limit our sympathies to this Western Continent.

And whatever may be urged against our making a naval demonstration in Turkish waters, there is a widespread feeling among our people that our guns could never thunder in a more righteous cause.

But, however that may be, no one among us can question that it is our sacred duty to give trumpet-tongued utterance to the righteous indignation of the whole American people against "the deep damnation of the taking-off" of our Armenian brothers by fiendish massacres. Not only so; we can give practical and substantial expression to our feeling by a prompt and generous response to the appeal that comes to us for food and clothing for our shivering and starving Armenian brethren whom the sword of the Turk as yet has spared.

The unspeakable Turk, who has been supposed to be stone-deaf to the voice of humanity, has been compelled to listen to the voice of a woman, and Clara

4

Barton, followed by the God-speeds of the whole civilized world, has pressed through the gates grudgingly set ajar, and with her for our almoner we are brought into helpful touch with our suffering fellow-Christians in the Orient.

Let the tide of sympathy surge through the gates of the Bosphorus with so mighty a volume that even the Turk shall feel, as never before, the throb of Nineteenth Century Christian life.

P. S. HENSON.

First Baptist Church, Chicago.

VILLAGE ARMENIANS.

INTRODUCTORY.

ARMENIAN TEACHER AND WIFE.*

AT ROME, during the first century after Christ, the great amphitheater, whose ruins are now the admiration of the world, was in the height of its glory. There, on a festal day, might be seen a gathering that the world could not surpass for splendor or horror. There, in his private box, surrounded with all magnificence, was the Emperor, brutal-eyed and sensual, looking with unconcealed ennui upon most spectacles, even those which excited the populace in a high degree. Around him were the Senators in their robes of office, and the Vestal virgins clad in white. A little farther away were the Knights, the wealthy men of Rome, and filling the remainder of the building were 18,000 of the "populus Romanus," who

* This gentleman is a college graduate, speaks and reads four languages with equal facility, and has assisted in the preparation of a lexicon. He was confined in prison for a year on a frivolous charge of treason. Both he and his wife are excellent Christian people.

7

must be appeased with "bread and shows," lest they overturn the government. Battles of gladiators from Thrace and Numidia, of ferocious beasts from India, and Africa, and the wilds of Germany and Dacia, naval battles in which the arena was flooded and men fought upon ships, dyeing the waters with human blood, furnished the realism, so thoroughly developed at that time. But nothing excited the interest of Emperor, or subject, or Senator, or Vestal, as when there was an announcement: "Christiani ad leones," the Christians to the lions! Then, when hoary sage or gentle matron, strong manhood or lovely maiden came forth to die, then there was interest! The great gates were opened; there would be a fierce rush of striped tiger or tawny lion, one feeble scream, a few fierce snarls, and all would be over. Then satisfaction would light up the bleared eyes of the Emperor; a shout of triumph goes up from the mighty multitude; the wild beasts are driven back to their dens, and all is finished. The next number of the program is called.

The world has seen a spectacle exceeding this in horror, during the years of 1894 and 1895. Christian men of education, women as tenderly reared, with instincts for purity as keen as in America, children with skins no darker and forms as fair as any in our own land, have seen their homes destroyed, their means of livelihood taken away, the bread-winners murdered with torture, and women and children subjected to treatment far worse than that of their proto-types before Nero. In place of one ignorant heathen emperor are the sovereigns of the six most powerful

8

and enlightened nations of Europe, all approving of this carnage and destruction by sitting and looking on, when it is in their power to say, " Hold, it is enough!" Greed, fanaticism, cruelty, and lust are stalking through the land of Armenia. Thousands have died in vindicating their religion;-tens of thousands are now homeless and destitute, while the nations of Europe look on either indifferently or applauding the monstrous spectacle. The world looks on a while; now it is becoming ancient history, and all are ready for a new sensation. The ignorance which reigns in this country and in Europe can be the only excuse for this hard-heartedness.

The aim of this little book is to tell the facts in so brief a space that all may know them.

HARPOOT COLLEGE AND MISSION BUILDINGS.

I.

THE REIGN OF ABDUL HAMID BEFORE THE MASSACRES.

FOR 600 years the Armenians were the most submissive servants of the Ottoman Empire, and the most prosperous of the non-Mohammedan races, Christians and Jews, who paid tribute as a penalty for not accepting Islam.

The accession of the present Sultan marked a change in their condition. He had not been long on the throne before a constantly increasing series of oppressions were begun. They had been the bankers and merchants of the country.

The reason for this course of action is not hard to seek. Sultan Abdul Hamid lost Bulgaria, a valuable part of his dominions, because of their prosperity and a spread of European ideas of liberty and European civilization among them. He feared that he would lose the Armenians also, if they became as prosperous and enlightened. He did not realize that the Armenians were not in a compact body as are the Bulgarians, that they are much farther from Europe, that they are in a minority everywhere of the population. Still less did he understand that the Armenians, as a race, had no national aspirations. A mercantile or agricultural people, their only desire was to peacefully pursue their avocations. Misled by his palace favorites, he only saw that the Armenians were increasing in wealth, in intelligence, and moral character. He only heard the voices of a few blatant revolutionists, who, from refuges in Russia, England, or America, were sending out silly manifestoes, urging the Armenians to insane rebellion, which could only result in their own destruction. Add to this a growing tendency upon the part of the Armenians to question in regard to their rights, and we have the reasons of the Sultan for this course of action.

PRELIMINARY PERSECUTIONS.

They were hampered by custom-house espionage and postal, passport, and quarantine regulations that tended to stifle trade, which were enforced in Armenian districts alone. The Armenians are industrious and successful farmers. Their agriculture was crushed by a system of taxation that prevented progress, and took all but the merest pittance from the tillers of the soil. They desired to improve their places of worship and build new ones, as well as to erect schools. They must apply to the ministry of public instruction to rebuild the fallen wall of a church, or to open a primary school or a branch in a different ward of the town. The permit must be signed by the Sultan himself, and in order to get it to his august presence, a hundred men must be bribed to do their duty. To present it at all, there must be unanimous testimony of the religious heads of all denominations that the school or church building is necessary and unobjectionable. In addition to these legalized wrongs there are innumerable illegal ones. Oppression, violence, and bribery impoverished and made the lives of the Armenians a burden.

About five years ago the Sultan discovered a new method of oppression. He organized the Kourds into regiments of cavalry, called from his own name, "Hamidieh." It was announced to the European ambassadors that the Sultan, ever mindful of the good of his people, and finding it difficult to restrain the ravages of the half-wild Kourds upon the defenseless Armenians, had determined to organize a number of regiments of irregular cavalry upon the model of the Russian Cossack regiments. They were to be officered from the regular army, and enrolled in regiments, so that it would be possible to locate every individual Kourd. In addition to this, according to the originator of this brilliant scheme, Shakir Pasha, who is now superintendent of reforms in Armenia, this Kourdish cavalry would make an excellent bulwark against the Russians on the Armenian frontier.

The results were not in accordance with the announcements. The Kourds were not officered from the regular army, but from their own chiefs, whose character can be judged from one example: Hussien Agha, chief of the Haidaranli Kourds, in the district of Patnotz, was appointed a colonel of this cavalry, and soon after promoted to the rank of brigadier-general, with the title of pasha. He had already signalized his fitness for such an office by a long course of pillage and arson in the helpless villages around him. When he was appointed colonel he was under charges from the British Consulate in Erzeroum. It had been proved against him that he had gone to an Armenian village and attacked a house in which there was a young girl whom he wished to abduct. The girl had hidden in a strawstack, and they were not able to find her. In order to force her out, they seized the girl's little brother and tortured him until his screams forced the sister to come out from her hiding place and give herself up. She was put in horrible slavery, from which it is not known that she ever escaped. This matter was brought to the attention of the Imperial Government at Constantinople, together with numberless other outrages. He was brought to Erzeroum for trial at one time, was kept there for some months, and sent back to his district, apparently acquitted. It is impossible to find that he was ever tried. This was in time of peace, before Armenian outrages began to startle the world.

The appointment of the Hamidieh cavalry marked a sad era to the Armenians. Both peoples understood the meaning of this move. When the Kourdish chiefs were at Erzeroum, the army headquarters, receiving their commission in the new cavalry, they went through the market brandishing their swords and saying to the Armenian merchants: "Go to the cemeteries, and dig your own graves, and bury yourselves. Heretofore we have robbed you and tormented you of our own free will; now, however, we have the instructions of His Imperial Majesty to do our will upon you. By burying yourselves now you will save us much trouble later." A thousand Armenians buried in one trench, in one day, in November, 1895, has fulfilled this grim prophecy.

14

The condition presaged by these remarks was soon in force all over Armenia. In 1890, the preacher of a Protestant church told his missionary, "Kourds near our districts are burning our fields. They say this year, your grain; next year, your flocks and cattle; the year after that, your daughters; and the year after that, yourselves we will take." They have kept their word. In a few years the provinces were decimated, Alashgerd, for instance, being almost entirely "purged" of Armenians. Over 20,000 woe-stricken wretches, once healthy and well-to-do, fled to Russia in rags and misery, deformed, diseased, or dying; on the way they were seized over and over again by soldiers of the Sultan, who deprived them of the little money they possessed, nay, of the clothes they were wearing; outraged the married women in the presence of their sons and daughters; deflowered the tender girls before the eyes of their mothers and brothers, and then drove them over the frontiers to hunger and die. Those who remained behind for a time were no better off. Kourdish brigands lifted the last cows and goats of the peasants, and carried off their carpets and their valuables. Turkish tax-gatherers followed these, gleaning what the brigands had left, and, lest anything should escape their avarice, bound the men, flogged them till their bodies were a bloody, mangled mass, cicatrized their wounds with red-hot ramrods, plucked out their beards hair by hair, and tore the flesh from their limbs with pincers.

This was their condition in time of peace, before there was any charge of Armenian rebellion.

II.

THE EARLIER MASSACRES.

The massacres are not, as may be thought from casual reading of the newspapers, of recent commencement. The first one was in Erzeroum, in June, 1890. The Armenians of that city were accused of making rifles and cannon in a small machine-shop which was a part of the manual-training department of a high school. An anonymous letter charged this, and that the arms were stored in the basement of the church next door. On this basis the Turkish officials came suddenly upon the school and church, placing a cordon of military around them. They went through all the buildings, ripping up floors and stairways to find hiding places for arms. When nothing was found, they went to the church and examined it thoroughly. Of course, nothing was found. The Armenians were so shocked by this violation of their holy place that they closed their shops and went to their cemeteries in large numbers, mourning its desecration. They were ordered to disperse, but, before they had time to do so, a battalion of troops had come upon them and fired upon them — with blank cartridges, it is claimed. However this may be, three were killed on the spot, and a mob of Turks, civilians, and soldiers rushed about the markets and residence streets shouting, "The gates of heaven are opened! Kill, my brother, kill!" Fifteen persons were killed; 300 were so badly wounded that many died of wounds or fright. There were over fifty Armenians arrested and kept in jail for months, where many died. The following spring, in token of the Sultan's most glorious majesty and clemency, they were released on condition that they might pray for life for him for a thousand years. No charge was ever preferred against them. No Turk was ever arrested participating in this riot.

After this, at intervals of a few months, massacres of this kind occurred at Caesarea, Yozgat, Marsovan, and some other towns, with a pause after each, as if to test the feelings of Europe. As nothing was done, the time was felt to be ripe for a stroke on a larger scale.

SASSOUN.

Sassoun is a district in Eastern Turkey, in the mountains southwest of Moosh. Its inhabitants were mountaineers, hardy and simple, tilling little patches on the mountain sides and keeping flocks and herds. After the inauguration of the Hamidieh cavalry the Kourds persecuted them, until at last it became impossible for them to pay taxes, as the Kourds robbed them of crops and live stock. They resisted the Kourds and killed a few. Regular infantry to the number of 5,000, assisted by three batteries of mountain guns and 900 artillerists, were sent from Erzeroum, Erzingan, Bitlis, Diarbekir, and Kharpoot. The villagers at once surrendered on seeing the uniforms of the regular troops. They were butchered wherever they could be caught. That so many escaped was entirely due to the sheltering rocks and brushwood that concealed any one who could get twenty feet away from his pursuers.

Thirty-five villages were plundered and burned; probably 1,000 were slain. Happy, however, were those merely slain. Women were outraged and then butchered. A priest who went to beg for mercy to his people had his eyes bored out, was scored on face, and breast, and limbs with the sign of the cross, and slowly hacked to pieces. Three children were tied together, in the presence of their mothers, and one soldier, on a wager, cut off the three heads with one stroke of his sword. Sixty women and girls were confined in one church; the soldiers were turned loose among them to work their brutal lust, and when this was satiated they were cut to pieces in every possible ingenuity of torture. Children were seized by two lusty Turks, and their legs pulled apart. Everything that Satanic lust, cruelty, and fanaticism could suggest was done. Outrages and tortures, too vile for the pages of a book in a Christian country, were daily perpetrated. When the news of this outrage slowly filtered out of the country, such an outcry came from outraged England that the British Government was forced to press for reforms.

Public opinion in England forced the government to demand an investigation, and a commission was appointed from the three embassies of England, France, and Russia, and sent to Moosh, which is the nearest city to Sassoun. The Turkish Government had already, in response to the demands of the ambassadors, sent a commission for investigation, but its work was discounted by a previous commission, which had been sent to decorate with high orders the commander-in-chief of the army which had operated against Sassoun. The commanders of the different regiments also received rewards and standards. The European delegates sat with the Turks and joined in the investigation, but made separate reports.

In this connection a bit of hitherto unwritten history will be of interest. When the Sultan found that he must send a commission of inquiry to Sassoun, some of whom must be foreigners, he sent for U. S. Minister Terrell and told him that the governments of Europe were infringing upon his sovereignty and were determined to send an extra-legal commission to investigate the suppression of the rebellion at that place.

This was at the time when Mr. Terrell had only been in the country a short time and had not learned, as he since has, the true inwardness of Turkish diplomacy. Coming directly from places of purely domestic responsibility, he was placed at a great disadvantage as compared with European diplomatists, who make this a life-long profession. The mistakes which Mr. Terrell made should not be charged to him, but to our diplomatic system, which is a century behind the times.

He asked Minister Terrell if the United States would help him out of a hard place, and desired that an American representative be sent with the commission as a member of it, thus forestalling the action of the European powers. He suggested, also, the name of a former agent of the United States who was suspected of having received bribes from the Turkish Government. As this man would be a member of the Turkish Commission, even if he desired to give a fair and independent report, he could not do so, as his Turkish colleagues would outvote him and prevent him from obtaining any independent witnesses. Minister Terrell sent this request on to Washington, containing this gentleman's name.

Within a few hours the British Embassy was informed of this action, and they at once sent for an American gentleman, a forty years' resident of Constantinople, who has the confidence of both the British and the United States governments. He was told of this action, and his advice was sought. At once understanding that if this American representative were sent, it would assist the Turkish Government in covering up the whole atrocious affair, he suggested that the British Foreign Office in London cable to Washington, indorsing the request of the Sultan and suggesting the name of another United States representative who is known everywhere for his probity, and, understanding the languages of the country, would be a check upon any attempt to whitewash the affair; also, that this representative be instructed to act, not as a member of the commission, but to make an independent investigation. The United States Government acted upon this suggestion, and shortly afterward it was made public that, in response to an invitation of the Turkish Government, Consul Jewett of Sivas was instructed to make this investigation. On the publication of this name the Turkish Government withdrew its invitation and refused to allow Mr. Jewett to go.

III.

THE REFORMS.

On the return of the commission, the representatives of France, Russia, and England presented their identical notes to the Porte, demanding that certain reforms be granted in six Armenian provinces : Van, Erzeroum, Sivas, Kharpoot, Bitlis, and Diarbekir. For four months the Sultan resisted these propositions, on various pretexts — among them, that there was nothing new in them, which was a fact, as the treaties and agreements of the last forty years had guaranteed them all repeatedly; on the grounds that there was no need of reforms; that concession of these reforms would be an invasion of his sovereignty, and that, however favorably disposed he might be under other circumstances to concede these reforms, he could not do it under compulsion; and the threats of the powers of active interference implied compulsion.

However, at the end of four months he conceded the reforms and appointed Shakir Pasha* as High Commissioner to carry them out. The concessions of the reforms marked a new period in Armenian history, this last and most bloody chapter.

---

*Shakir Pasha was the man who suggested the organization of the Hamidieh Cavalry, and was more responsible than any person, except the Sultan himself, for its organization and the resulting abuses and outrages.

Reforms shall be inaugurated in the six provinces as follows:

First. The Governor Generals, "*Valis.*" Endeavor shall be made to reduce the number of these so that there shall be more dignity attaching to the office. They shall hold office for five years, or during good behavior. The Ottoman Government should semi-officially acquaint the embassies with the persons to be appointed to this office. These Governor Generals shall have Christian assistants if they are Mohammedans, and vice versa. The assistants of the Governor Generals shall receive petitions, supervise persons and police, and control collections and taxes.

Second. The Sub-Governors (Mutsessariff and Kaimakam). At least one-third of these officials in each province shall be Christians. When they are Mohammedans they shall have Christian assistants, and vice versa.

Third. Provincial Councils. Each of these three classes of Governors shall have a council composed of members equally divided between two faiths, who shall enjoy full confidence of their respective peoples. There shall be two Christians and two Mohammedans, presided over by the Governor in this council. No paid official of the Governor shall be a member of this council.

Fourth. The most crying abuses in the villages and communes are remedied. The new regulations are that a rural police shall be recruited from Turks and Christians alike, and that from these two-thirds of the gendarmerie or police shall be gathered, the remainder from the regular army. The Christian villages, so far as practicable, shall be set apart in separate communes. No member of a village, commune, or council shall hold any other office.

Fifth. Tithes and taxes shall be levied by the communal chiefs and councils. No "tax farming" to be allowed.* No soldiers or police are to be quartered on the people gratuitously.

Sixth. There shall be certain reforms of the courts of justice on the basis of making them more efficient and impartial.

Seventh. A High Commissioner shall be appointed by the Sultan and approved by the powers, with an assistant who shall be a Christian if the former is a Mohammedan, with authority over the Governor Generals of the provinces. He shall make full inspection of the provinces, and may amend measures which may not be in conformity with the new regulations.

Eighth. A permanent committee of control shall be established, to sit in Constantinople. This body shall oversee all the reforms proposed above. It shall be composed of three Mohammedans and three Christians and be presided over by high civil or military officials. The embassies shall communicate directly with this body through their dragomans on the subject of reforms.'

RECORD OF EVENTS

From the demand for reform to the beginning of the Reign of Terror:

May 11 — Scheme of reforms presented.

June 10 — The Sultan's cabinet changed, and time requested for them to study the new proposition.

June 15 — More delays requested.

---

* The customary system in Turkey is to have the taxes sold to the highest bidder, and they collect from the people what they can, sometimes less, usually much more, than the legal amount.

ASIA MI

SMYRNA

Dugis

Koneck

Adalia

Koraman

Mazon

Rhodes

CYPRUS

MEDITERRANEAN

SEA

MAP OF

ARMENIA

JRKEY IN ASIA

WNS UNDERLINED ARE SCENES OF MASSACRE

June 17 — Reforms accepted in form, but discussion of certain points requested. Objection made to ratification of high commissioners appointed by the powers. Guarantees refused.

June 19 — The request for discussion of certain points acceded to. The dragomans go to the Minister of Foreign Affairs and ask to have the points for further discussion named. Although they remained five hours, the only reply made is that the minister can not add anything to what he has already said.

June 22 — The fall of the Rosebery ministry. Delays. Further negotiations.

June 27 — Porte appoints Shakir Pasha inspector without consultation with the powers, or power to act independently. He can only make reports.

June 29 — The Porte appoints a commission to recommend reforms.

July 3 — This commission announces that it does not know what points in the scheme of reform are reserved for discussion.

July 15 — The commission makes a report which is not made public.

July 19 — The Porte reports to the ambassadors that a scheme of reforms "will be reported shortly."

July 20 — Firm language from Lord Salisbury to the Turkish Ambassador in London results in Shakir Pasha being instructed to superintend reforms. " A good impression is made."

July 22 — Announcement made that the Porte will communicate its reply on Armenian reforms the following day.

July 23 — Firman is issued, granting amnesty to political prisoners, except those accused of other crimes.

August 1 — A cabinet council decides that the scheme of reforms shall apply to all the Empire.

August 4 — The reply of the Porte to the demands of the powers is made public. In non-essential matters it agrees with the scheme proposed by the powers. The articles which give force to the latter are omitted.

August 6 — The French and Russian embassies reject the Turkish scheme of reform.

August 7 — The dragomans of the three embassies are called to the Porte and are assured that the reforms will be carried out. The Porte is surprised to learn that its scheme is unsatisfactory. The Armenian Patriarch asks that aid be sent to the Armenian sufferers in Sassoun through the American missionaries. The Sultan orders $8,800 distributed among Sassoun sufferers.

August 13 — The embassies present a collective note on Armenian reforms to the Porte, demanding more explicit statement of certain points which are utterly incomprehensible in the last Turkish reply.

August 18 — The Porte defines reforms which it has accepted for Armenia. They are considered of only slight importance, as the principle of foreign aid is rejected. The ambassadors report to their governments.

August 25 — Shakir Pasha, who had been appointed two months before, starts for Erzeroum. He is accompanied by a commission consisting entirely of Mohammedans. The ambassadors ignore this step, as they expect no practical results therefrom.

August 27 — The Ottoman Government complains to those of Paris and St. Petersburg of the discourtesy of Great Britain in keeping her fleet at the mouth of the Dardanelles. Replies to this communication are not favorable.

August 28 — The Porte names certain concessions in the evening and at midnight withdraws them.

September 27 — Concessions again made, but vital points are still withheld

September 30 — A large number of Armenians in Constantinople go to the Porte with a petition for redress of grievances. They are attacked by police on the way; a major of police is killed, as are many Armenians. The Turkish official account of this occurrence was as follows: " At the instigation of certain Armenian agitators disorderly groups gathered in front of the Patriarchate, but thanks to the measures taken by the authorities, order continues to be maintained." According to this account about eighty Armenians were killed, of whom one was a woman. The diplomatic body of Constantinople issued the following supplementary account of this occurrence in a note: 1. Private persons aroused by the police were beaten and killed without the police taking any steps to protect them. 2. Orderly persons without arms were attacked by Turks, beaten, and killed. The wounded were taken to the courts, and prisoners killed in cold blood.

October 1 — Another change of ministry. Kiamil Pasha, leader of the Turks in favor of reform, appointed to be Grand Vizier.

October 4 — Bahri Pasha fired upon in Trebizond.

October 8 — The massacre of Trebizond. See page 29.

October 10 — Reply is received from the Porte to the note of the diplomatic body state that the Armenians were to be blamed entirely for the outbreak of September 30th. " The reply is not considered satisfactory."

October 17 — The reforms as called for by the powers are conceded. Representations are received that the Christians in Asia Minor are being disarmed and the Mohammedans supplied with weapons.

October 21 — Massacre in Erzeroum. About 900 Armenians killed.

October 25 — Massacre at Baiboort and its villages. Armenian school raided. Teachers and children killed.

October 30 — Erzeroum massacre. See pages 29-31. This was followed by others in quick succession.

IV.

THE REIGN OF TERROR.

WHEN all was ready, the match was put to the train. Within a week from the acceptance of the reforms the blow, carefully prepared, fell with crushing force on the Armenians. October 8th a massacre occurred at Trebizond, which resulted in the death of about 500 Armenian men, the pillaging of their houses and shops, and the reduction of 1,000 families to beggary at the beginning of winter. From Trebizond the tidal wave of massacre rapidly rolled up over the mountains of Armenia. Gumush-Khana, Baiboort, and its villages were next attacked. At the latter place the Armenian children were set upon in their parochial school, and teachers and pupils involved in one fate.

THE ARMENIAN PATRIARCH OF CONSTANTINOPLE.

THE EXPERIENCE OF ERZEROUM.

October 30th the movement reached Erzeroum at 9.30 a. m. "We were surprised," said one who afterward told the story, "as morning drill was over, when

VICTIMS OF THE ERZEROUM MASSACRES.
(From a Photograph.)

we were drawn up, our arms and ammunition were examined, and we were told to prepare for active work. We were then dismissed, and soon after noon prayer (12.30 p. m.) the bugle sounded again. We had sharpened our sword bayonets and filled our cartridge belts. We were told that the Armenians were in rebellion, that we were to attack and sack the Armenian quarter, to kill all men, and the booty of all kinds should be ours." Too well they obeyed orders. The bugle sounded "Begin firing," and with a wild rush the soldiers fell on the defenseless Armenian quarter next the barracks. During the next four hours 560 Armenians, mostly men, were killed, and but sixty were wounded. The southeast quarter of the city, a district three-fourths of a mile long and half a mile wide, was absolutely devastated, every house but three belonging to Armenians being looted; every removable article was removed; the doors, windows, and heavy articles were smashed with axes or hammers. In one house a fine piano, too heavy to be removed, was smashed to kindling wood with axes. The bazaars fared as badly as the houses. More than half of the thousand Armenian shops were looted.

One street, on which were some of the best, for some unexplained reason, escaped. Here in Erzeroum ghastly incidents and hair-breadth escapes were not lacking. Our illustration on page 30 gives one sad case: A mother and her two little ones were killed together, while the former was fighting for her honor. The woman's form was not in a condition to be photographed. This is from a photograph taken on the spot the day after the deed. One house containing a dozen women and girls, with that of two neighbors, was guarded by one of the Turks, who, though a thoroughly unprincipled man, filled his own house with spoil of other houses in the expectation of reward, swore that these three houses belonged to Mohammedans, and thus saved them. The father and two sons in this family were in their shop in the market. They barricaded themselves inside and went below into a sort of a coal cellar. While there they heard four soldiers come in and begin throwing their goods about; then they broke open the safe where there was a thousand pounds in gold ($5,000). At the sight of the gold they began quarreling as to who should have it. One, an officer, claimed it all and shot one of the soldiers; the others then fled, and this officer gathered up the gold in a cloth and made away with it. After this the rabble came in and looted the place. After these had gone the three men dug into an adjoining cellar, and thence into the next one, which belonged to a friendly Turk, who kept them two days and then took them home.

The sudden outburst of the massacre found Rev. W. N. Chambers coming home from the telegraph office, where he had just been to send a dispatch saying all was quiet. While in the market the riot began. Though fired at a dozen times he was mercifully preserved and ran home with many others. The mission house sheltered 400 people that night, many of them women whose houses had been destroyed and who only looked for the morning to bring them their dead.

Two days after, 560 bodies were buried together in the Armenian cemetery.

The massacres continued for about six weeks and swept over Armenia from north to south, from the Black Sea to the Mediterranean and Mesopotamia. Let some of those present in these places tell the story.

THE HARPOOT HORROR.

We escaped from our houses with our lives with a crowd of people who had taken refuge in our yard and house. Four of the company were wounded as they were fleeing from our houses, while a shower of bullets, fired by soldiers and Turks from Martini rifles, whistled over their heads, and numbers struck Mr. Gates' house. These shots were fired from the spot where the soldiers were stationed with a cannon. A cannon shot passed through the narrow passage through which the crowd was fleeing, and buried itself in a wall. A bombshell was fired from a point between Mezire and the city and entered Doctor Barnum's study through a window, bending a stout iron rod, plowed through the side of a bookcase, and exploded about five feet from the place where it entered, and struck in over twenty places, gouging deep holes in the walls. Doctor Barnum and family fled from the room only a short time before this bomb was fired; otherwise, it might have killed them all, with others who were with them in the room. It appears that other bombs were fired and burst in other houses, and also solid shot in others. If any one says the Martini bullets were fired by Kourds, we have only to show by marks on the walls that they came from where the soldiers were stationed with a cannon. How will they explain the firing of cannon with bombs? These were in the hands of soldiers, and they directed their fire according to the orders of their superiors.

We have lost everything — account books, deeds of property ; our safe was broken open, money taken; not a scrap of paper or memorandum of anything, besides hundreds of books and papers which never can be replaced.

Another letter gives a tabulated statement with particulars of the destruction in 170 places in the Harpoot district.

Samples are the following :

AIVOSH.— Seventy women killed. This place wiped out. Women and girls carried off. Priest forced to sound the "call to prayer," then shot. He blessed the man who shot him, then said, " Shoot me again."

ARABKIR.— Two thousand killed. Pastor and others killed in prison. Plunder complete. Even the richest are destitute.

CHUNKUSH.— One hundred and three houses burned ; six hundred and eighty people killed. November 4th, Kourds plundered the market and withdrew, but returned at night and burned eighty-three houses. Christians taken to a mosque and forced to accept Islam. Gave up weapons. November 18th, Kaimakam (local governor) came. November 14th, Kourds returned ; soldiers fired on Christians, and Kourds then raided the town. All armed with Martini rifles. Protestant church, school, and parsonage burned.

DIARBEKIR.— Two thousand killed November 1-3. Began by Moslems issuing from a mosque and burning the market. Christians defended themselves. Do not know how many Turks were slain.

HUELI.— Two hundred and sixty-three houses burned ; ninety people killed. All but thirty-seven poor houses burned. Seventy-five Protestant houses and their fine new Protestant house burned. Two priests killed. The last houses burned were kindled with kerosene sent by the Government. Survivors accepted Islam or are fugitives.

HUSENIK.— Nine houses burned; two hundred and sixty killed; two hundred wounded. Many of the dead were shot by soldiers. List of killed still increasing. Priests killed with great indignity.

KONK.— Three hundred Armenians and the Protestant pastor killed. Church a mosque, chapel a sheepfold.

34

MALATIA.— Fifteen hundred Armenian houses. Five thousand killed. "Worse than Habusi." No details.

PERI.— Four hundred Armenian houses. Eight killed; twelve wounded. Agha took people to his house for "protection," while Kourds plundered the village; then he sent them back. Gathered leading men to take them to Palu for circumcision. Outside the village ten were shot. Under the lead of a Christian woman, fifty-five men, women, and children threw themselves into the river.

SHEIKHAJI.— November 5th and 6th. Saved by Agha on payment of twenty liras. All became Moslems. Two priests killed — one with great indignity. Haji Bey and his son Mustapha were foremost in destroying the village. Now Agha gives a woman to each soldier and zaptiah on guard every night. He has given two married women to his son and two to renegade Armenians.

Still later comes the following summary of events in this province:

```
Killed .......................................... 30,601
Burned to death ................................. 1,436
Preachers and priests killed ....................    51
Died from starvation ............................ 2,461
Died unprotected in the fields .................. 4,340
Died from fear ..................................   660
Wounded ......................................... 8,000
Houses burned ...................................28,545
Forcible conversions ............................15,066
Women and girls abducted ........................ 5,546
Forcible marriages .............................. 1,551
Churches burned .................................   227
Destitute and starving ..........................94,750
```

THE SORROWS OF SIVAS.

From a resident and eye-witness:

" Do not believe that in Sivas was other than an unprovoked attack upon business men in their shops, innocent women and children in their homes, and even

35

upon the school-houses, in which hundreds of children were assembled. Thanks be to God, our school gates did not give way under the repeated murderous assaults, and by 4.30 p. m. Mr. Perry, accompanied by a guard, was able to escort most of the 400 pupils home. The streets were in the hands of murderous looters, whose wives and children assisted in stripping the dead and robbing the houses.

"The market became a slaughter-pen and the shops booty. The threefold signal, a sort of buzz from the criers on the minarets, and a trumpet call, was given, and understood only by plotters and executioners, and in an instant merchant and patron, citizen and villager, whoever was in sight or reach, was beset either by a 'Karsman'* with a heavy club, Circassian with knife and revolver, or by soldier with Martini rifle.

"Bear with me while I tell you of our dear native pastor. He was in the shop of one of his church members, who occupied a room on the first floor of a large building, the upper stories of which were used for various purposes. When this merchant saw that the soldiers upon whom they had depended for help had joined in with the massacre and looting, he and his partner fled to the roof, calling for the pastor to follow them. In the excitement of the moment, however, he either did not hear the call or did not understand, and separating from his friends he made his way quickly to an upper room whither many others had fled. They were quickly followed by the robbers, who took what money they had on their persons. They were then left unharmed by violence. The terrible work of killing men in the streets was continued till dark. Of course this prevented those who had taken refuge in various rooms upstairs from leaving. Through those dreadful hours our pastor found himself surrounded by

---

* These are Mohammedan refugees from the district about Kars, who settled in the Sivas district after Kars was ceded to Russia.

an audience who, together with himself, stood face to face with death. He prayed with them, preached to them, and did everything he could to comfort them. About an hour or two before dark, soldiers went to these upper rooms. When the soldiers reached them they offered life to the pastor on condition that he would renounce Christianity and accept Mohammedanism. He refused to do so and was struck. The offer was repeated, and again he refused, and he was smitten the second time. The offer was made the third time. Looking his assailants in the face he replied: 'Not only am I a believer in the religion of Christ, but for years I have been a preacher of it. I can not give it up. If you wish to kill me for this, I am ready.' Lifting his hands toward heaven in token of acceptance he fell, twice pierced with rifle balls. He leaves a devoted wife and four lovely daughters, all of whom were dependent upon their natural protector for support."

From another letter:

"As the fury of this storm of blood and greed subsided the stricken Armenians of Sivas slowly gathered the mangled and naked bodies of their kinsmen to their cemetery, where a great trench had been dug to hold the harvest of death. A single priest read a short service over the long and ghastly rank, and thus was closed another chapter in the yet unfinished story of cruelty, lust, and fanaticism.

"It is a fact, I think, that the Kaimakam (Governor) of Gurun telegraphed to the Vali (Governor General) at Sivas, saying in effect: 'You may rest assured that there is not an Armenian left in Gurun.' The Armenians in Gurun made some resistance to being butchered, and suffered worse for it. Gurun is a large village about twenty-four hours from Sivas. It has a population of 10,000, one-half Armenians.

"The Armenian villagers in the vicinity have been

37

robbed of everything, and the people are left to beg and die. The suffering on the approach of winter will be very great. Food is scarce. Everything was carried off from the Armenian shops. There will be an immense amount of suffering all over the country."

In Kutterbul, a suburb of Diarbekir, the Protestant pastor was killed in the presence of his wife. His wife, who was with her child, five years old, and sister were carried away by the Kourds. This woman saw her children, one two years old, the other but a few months, thrown into the street, where they died. She also saw the Kourds pouring kerosene over a man and setting fire to him. Another woman and two little ones were left in the rain without one rag to cover them. Her husband also was killed.

THE BLOODY BAPTISM OF BITLIS.

The following is from a gentleman whose home is in Bitlis:

"The massacre at Bitlis began in the market. Perhaps you know the place. Very few escaped death. My brother, who, with his wife, was a graduate of Harpoot College, was principal of the boys' high-school and dragoman (interpreter) of the British Vice Consulate in Moosh. He went to the market at the noon recess and was slaughtered most cruelly and his naked body found six days later. During the intervening time friends could not search for or bury their dead. My uncle S. was shot and dragged by the mob and massacred in the massacre in the market. My younger brother was wounded two weeks after the massacre but recovered. My poor father was not at market at the time of the slaughter; he was at the house of a friend. Afterward he applied to the government for a guard to take him safely home. He was arrested and is still (January 18th) in prison. They are still in danger and unsafe. The poverty at Bitlis is awful. Some are starving—dying of hunger. Our family have only dry bread. Oh, dear me! What will be our condition?"

The family spoken of here were among the wealthiest and most aristocratic in Bitlis. They, like many others, are reduced to penury.

Particulars could be given of many other places, but it will be sufficient to merely give their names—Trebizond, Gumush-Khana, Baiboort, Erzeroum, Bitlis, Palu, Harpoot, Arabkir, Malatia, Gurun, Sivas, Marsovan, Cæsarea, Diarbekir, Marash, Aintab, Oorfa, Roum-Kaleh, Sert Jezireh, Erzingan, Geghi, Kamakh, and Hassan-Kaleh. Besides these towns, hundreds of villages were the scenes of pillage and massacre.

SUMMARY.

Leaving out the massacre of September in Constantinople — see "Summary of Events"—and that of Trebizond, which were in some slight sense provoked by indiscreet Armenians, a series of massacres began simultaneously with the publication of the grant of reforms. They were in no place incited by any act, overt or otherwise, of the Armenians. They swept the whole country of Armenia, from north to south, and were rigidly confined in the limits of the six provinces. Where marauders tried to extend their work beyond these limits, they were sternly turned back by the military. The massacre closed about December 24th with an especially atrocious outbreak upon Oorfa, where 3,500 persons sealed their faith in blood.

PRESENT STATUS OF THE "REFORMED PROVINCES."

The whole country is desolate. Everywhere the Armenians are in want of food, clothing, furniture, and bedding. The prominent men are everywhere killed or impoverished; the poor are utterly destitute. Depending on the rich for employment, in the cessation of business and the losses which their employers have sustained, they are dependent entirely on the gifts of the charitable for food, clothing, and bedding.

V.

WHO IS TO BLAME?

1. His Imperial Majesty, Abdul Hamid II, the Shadow of God, the Refuge of the World, the Father of Sovereigns, the Man-Slayer, the Lord of Two Seas and Three Continents.

This is a grave charge, but which can be substantiated. It can not be thrown off on subordinates, for as none of those concerned in the massacre of Sassoun were punished, as no Moslem concerned in any of these outbreaks has been imprisoned, and as he is absolute monarch with power to do so, it can fairly be judged that he can not be held clear of this guilt. But proofs are more positive than this.

The Sultan's consent to the Reforms, delayed from May 11 to October, marks the time which was necessary to organize massacre on so large a scale. Omitting those at Constantinople and Trebizond, where events were precipitated by hot-headed Armenians, the massacres began simultaneously with the granting of

ABDUL HAMID II.

reforms, at Baiboort, at the extreme north of the provinces, extended in constantly increasing destruction at the southern limit. They were limited, also, in time to a few hours or days, began in many cases with the sound of trumpets, and ceased the same way. Outbreaks before or after the set time were as quickly suppressed as those outside the six provinces. They began everywhere at noon. Everywhere the Armenians were assured of safety and in many places were carefully disarmed before the massacres.

However, the most absolute proof was at Diarbekir. There the riots continued several days without hindrance. There the French Consul's life was threatened, and he telegraphed his Ambassador at Constantinople. Although the dispatch was received at night, he went at once to the Grand Vizier and demanded that the massacre stop so that his Consul should be safe. Further, he intimated that if the Consul was injured, the head of the Governor-General should be the forfeit, and that to enforce this the French fleet would be ordered to take Alexandria in twelve hours. Before the time was expired, a dispatch came announcing the complete restoration of tranquillity.

2. THE MOSLEM SPIRIT OF FANATICISM

That is everywhere ready to spring at the Christian is evident from the following MOHAMMEDAN PRAYER, which is used throughout Turkey, and daily repeated in the Cairo "Azhar" University by ten thousand Mohammedan students from all lands. The following translation is from the Arabic:

" I seek refuge with Allah from Satan (the *rejeem*), the accursed. In the name of Allah the Compassionate, the Merciful! O Lord of all Creatures! O Allah! Destroy the infidels and polytheists, thine enemies, the enemies of the religion! O Allah! Make their children orphans and defile their abodes! Cause their feet to slip; give them and their families, their households and their women, their children and their relations by marriage, their brothers and their friends, their possessions and their race, their wealth and their lands as booty to the Moslems, O Lord of all Creatures."

The following official death certificate is not an isolated one. It is transcribed from a British Consular report:

" We certify to the priest of the church of Mary (in an Armenian village) that the impure, stinking, putrid carcass of Sardeh, damned this day, may be allowed to putrify underground that it may no longer defile the air."

3. THE GOVERNMENTS OF EUROPE.

Especially England and Russia. Were it not for the jealousies of these two powers, Turkey would only be a reminiscence on the map of the world. Russia would long since have put a stop to these massacres had the Treaty of San Stefano continued in force, as this gave her power to superintend the Armenian Provinces; but England became the champion of Turkey, and, by the Treaty of Cyprus, became responsible for good conduct in Armenia, pledging herself to defend Turkey against Russia. Subsequently the Treaty of Berlin vested the supervision of reforms in the six signatory powers.

43

On the other hand, if Russia had acted in good faith during the past year, and had co-operated loyally with England, Turkey would have yielded in fact as in name, and the massacres would never have taken place.

The chronological statement of the diplomatic farce played at Constantinople during the summer shows well that Turkey knew she had some backing. It is now evident that the Czar was backing the Sultan; thus the blood of the innocent slain cries from the ground to these two great Christian (?) powers. They were accomplices before the fact, and are now accomplices after it.

4. THE ARMENIAN REVOLUTIONISTS.

For some years there has been in existence a number of revolutionary societies among the Armenians, whose efforts would be laughable, if their results had not been so disastrous—pitiable if they were not so reprehensible. But here again the hand of the Czar is evident. These societies were fostered in Russia. To the certain knowledge of the writer, rifles were sold on the Russian frontier of Armenia, at less than cost, with the express stipulation that they be sent into Turkey. Russian emissaries in disguise wandered about, stirring up strife and baseless hopes of independence to be won by the help of Russian Armenians. Stories were constantly set afloat by these miscreants that a large Armenian army, whose numbers grew with the distance from the frontier, was on the point of invading Turkey. Periodicals were published in Athens, Marseilles, and London, to stir up this revolutionary spirit.

This movement had no following among respectable, successful Armenians. Only irresponsible youths were with it, though the Turkish Government made these agitators and the few overt acts which they committed the excuse, not only for the massacres of Sassoun, but for all that has been done since.

DISTRIBUTION OF RELIEF IN AN ERZEROUM VILLAGE.

VI.

SOME BRIGHT SPOTS ON THE DARK PICTURE.

How dark this picture is, in which Moslem fanaticism and cruelty is mingled with the indifference and selfishness of so-called Christian nations; it is relieved a little by the heroism of those who are striving to alleviate the condition of the sufferers.

MISS CLARA BARTON.

Sir Philip Currie, the British Ambassador in Constantinople, has said that the only bright spot in all this darkness is the courage and devotion of the American missionaries; though in imminent danger of their lives, they have everywhere stood to their posts, and, at the conclusion of the massacres, stood ready to offer assistance to the victims, as far as means were afforded to do so.

Another example of heroism not less marked is that of Miss Clara Barton, at an age when most would consider themselves entitled to rest from toil, going at the first call, to relieve the suffering.

At Trebizond, on the sea-coast, and all through the interior, thousands are being aided at an expense of from four to ten cents per week each. In many cases a little bedding is being given to those who have lost everything. In Trebizond from sixty to eighty quilts are being dealt out, at the rate of one quilt to four persons. These are made at an expense of forty cents each.

At the latest advices the Turkish Government was putting no obstacles in the way of this work.

Acknowledgments are due to the following firms enabling it to be published at a nominal price:

J. W. BUTLER PAPER CO.,
BRADNER SMITH & CO.,
CHICAGO PAPER CO.,
AMERICAN PAPER CO.,
ILLINOIS PAPER CO.,
PAPER.

R. R. DONNELLY & SONS CO., The Lakeside Press,
PRESS-WORK AND BINDING.

GARDEN CITY ENGRAVING CO.,
J. MANZ & CO.,
THE STANDARD,
THE ADVANCE,
FARM, FIELD, AND FIRESIDE,
ENGRAVINGS.

RAND, McNALLY & CO.,
SPECIAL RATE ON COMPOSITION.

A YOUNG KURDISH CHIEF.

www.ingramcontent.com/pod-product-compliance
Lightning Source LLC
Chambersburg PA
CBHW022040080426
42733CB00007B/913